REVELATION
Seven Letters to Seven Churches

Linda Osborne

Copyright © 2014 Linda Osborne

All rights reserved.

Catch The Vision! Press

504 A Harbor View Drive, Klamath Falls, OR 97601

ISBN:-10: 0615977324
ISBN-13: 978-0615977324

CONTENTS

	Preface	i
1	Lesson 1	3
2	Lesson 2	12
3	Lesson 3	23
4	Lesson 4	35
5	Lesson 5	46
6	Lesson 6	55
7	Lesson 7	66
8	Lesson 8	77
9	Lesson 9	87
	About the Author	98

PREFACE

We are about to embark on an incredible journey! A journey which will take us from the rocky Island of Patmos on the Aegean Sea to a scenic view of the seven selected churches of Asia Minor, from which we will get a vantage point of the seven stages of church history. From there we will look beyond to some of the more significant and inspiring aspects of this unique book of the Bible, which gives us a view of our exciting future, catching a glimpse in each lesson of our glorified Lord and Savior Jesus Christ.

We will be looking predominantly at the first three chapters of this book, the letters to the seven churches of Asia Minor. We will not limit our lessons only to these letters, however, but will have Revelation as a whole in our view. As you begin your study, always pray that the Holy Spirit will enlighten you and apply God's word where it is needed. The theme Scripture for this study is, *"He who has an ear, let him hear what the Spirit says to the churches."* Revelation 2:7

We will lay the foundation of this exciting *final* book of the Bible as we look into the opening chapter ...

LESSON 1
REVELATION 1:1-8

Day 1

Read Revelation 1:1-3

1. Verse 1 begins by telling us the most important thing about this book and actually explains its name. What is this book, according to verse 1a?

The book of Revelation is called an apocalyptic book. The word *apocalypse* is the Greek word for *revelation* and means *uncovering, revealing* or *unveiling*. It is an unveiling *of that which otherwise could not be known.*

    a. Who, according to this title, is to be revealed as we study this book?

Charles Feinberg calls Revelation, *"God's final unveiling of the glories of His blessed Son,"* and tells us that, *"Our focus must ever be on Him in this Grand Finale."* Warren Wiersbe says, *"Whatever you do as you study this book, get to know the Savior better!"*

    b. Why don't we begin this study with a prayer asking God to reveal His Son to us anew as we study Revelation? This is a prayer we can be sure He will answer!

2. Within this revelation of the glorious Christ, what else will be revealed to us? (v. 1)

a. Why is it that these things are important to us? (When will these things take place?) How does verse 3b agree with this?

b. How do you feel about the Lord coming quickly?

3. Verse 1 tells us that several people were involved in the revelation given here. The revelation was given:

from
to
to
to
to

John MacArthur says, "As a reward for Christ's perfect submission and atonement, the Father now presented to Him the great record of His future glory. *Readers eavesdrop on the gift of this book, from the Father to His Son!*" (Emphasis mine.)

4. According to verse 2, to what three things did John bear witness?

a. Who is this John? v. 1b (See John 13:23; 21:24 and 1 John 1:1-3)

5. Revelation is the only book with the promise of a blessing. What must one do to receive this blessing? v. 3

LESSON 1

As an overview of today's study we see that this book is:

✟ The Revelation of *Jesus Christ*
✟ To show His bond-servants (us!) *the things which must shortly take place*
✟ Because *the time is near ...*

This week's memory verse:
"Behold, He is coming with clouds...even so, come, Lord Jesus."
Revelation 1:7; 22:20 NKJ

Day 2

Read Revelation 1:4-6

1. Although we see Revelation as a prophetic book, it is also an epistle! Who, again, is writing this letter? To whom is it written?

These were the seven selected churches located in the Roman province of Asia—actually Asia Minor, which today is Turkey. These seven churches were connected by a triangular highway and are named in their geographical order beginning with Ephesus, the most prominent, and going in a clockwise direction ending with Laodicea. Most likely this letter was carried along this same route and given out in the same order as it was written.

John would have been well known in this area, as he had spent much of his life and ministry in Ephesus.

2. John gives a two-fold salutation to the seven churches. What two words of Christian hope are given in his opening words to the churches?

a. What do you understand about the grace of God? (For those mature in your study of Scripture, share a verse which explains God's grace to you.)

b. What does God's peace mean to you? (See if you can think of a Scripture which best defines this peace.)

Of course, John himself cannot give grace and peace to the reader of this letter, so we see that it is God in Three Persons—the Trinity—as described in verses 4-5 from whom these gifts emanate.

3. For each Person of the Triune God write John's description (v.4-5):

✤ *God*

a. Warren Wiersbe speaks of God in this description as the *Eternal One*. How do the first four words of the Bible, found in Genesis 1:1 confirm the eternal nature of God?

✤ *The Holy Spirit*

b. Ephesians 4:4 tells us there is **one Spirit**. Isaiah 11:2 describes the sevenfold character of the Holy Spirit. From this verse, list these seven attributes of the Holy Spirit's character: (example) 1. *the Spirit of the Lord*

LESSON 1

✠ *Jesus Christ* (share the three names or descriptions given)

4. The three descriptions of Jesus Christ found in verse 5a give us a beautiful sense of the completeness of His ministry. With each of the following "names" see what the Scripture references have to say about Jesus:

   a. *The faithful witness*—John 14:6 and 9

   b. *The first-born of the dead*—1 Corinthians 15:20; Colossians 1:18

   c. *The ruler of the kings of the earth*—Philippians 2:9-10; Revelation 19:16

5. The book of Revelation is not only *about* Jesus Christ, it is dedicated *to* Him! Again, we have three descriptions—this time of what He has done *for us.* Fill in the following blank spaces from verses 5-6:

   ✠ *To Him who*_____
   What does it mean to you personally that Jesus Christ loves you? Do you really realize that He loves you?

   ✠ *To Him who*_____
   See what Titus 3:5 has to say about the cleansing of your sins.

✝ To Him who___________________________________

Read 1 Peter 2:9. What are we according to this verse?

1 Peter 2:10 goes on to say, *"... for you once were not a people, but now you are the people of God; you had not received mercy, but now you have received mercy."*

We sing a song that says, *No greater love has ever been or ever will be shown, that a man would die, lay down His life and give it for His friends;* and another that says, *Do you know what the blood has done for me, do you know what the blood has done for me? It has cleansed me; it has set me free ... do you know what the blood has done for me? Thank you Jesus, thank you Savior, for coming and washing me, coming and cleansing me, coming and setting me, setting me free!*

John finishes his thoughts at this high point with a doxology of praise to His Lord. It is surely understandable! You may wish to do the same!

Review this week's memory verse.

Day 3

Read Revelation 1:7-8

1. With what wonderful word of hope does John finish his salutation? v. 7a

The word behold means *look! Look, He is coming with the clouds!* The Children's Living Bible paraphrases it this way: *"See, He is arriving, surrounded by clouds."*

2. The Lord's coming is a keynote of the Book of Revelation. It is one of the first words in the book, and the last word is John's prayer that it would be soon! Each of the following verses in Revelation speak of the fact that *Jesus Christ is coming again*: 2:25; 3:3; 3:11; 16:15; 22:7; 22:12; 22:20. Read each one and share anything the Lord may reveal to you.

   a. Over and over again in these verses, Jesus tells us something about His coming. What is it?

   b. What are some of the things He says we should do because of His soon return?

3. John tells us that Jesus is coming in the clouds. What does Matthew 24:30b tell us about this fact?

   a. Read the exciting account in Acts 1:9-11 with this thought in mind. What is promised here?

   b. **Challenge**: Who would have been among this group of people watching Jesus depart in the clouds into heaven?

4. *How many* people will see Jesus when He comes, according to Revelation 1:7?

a. What particular people are included in this count?

b. From Zechariah 12:10, share how it will be when *those who pierced Him* see Him and recognize Him as Messiah.

Our Scripture passage today ends with words which have been ascribed to both God the Father and God the Son. *"'I am the Alpha and the Omega,' says the Lord God, 'who is and who was and who is to come, the Almighty.'"* Because of the Triune nature of God, they could have been spoken by either one. Though many see them as words of God, in the context of our book it seems more probable that they were said by Jesus.

Review this week's memory verse.

Day 4

Overview of Revelation 1:1-8

In this section we will be looking at the passage we have studied this week as a whole. The goal is to find the main lessons the Lord has for us from this chapter. Don't worry about being clever or profound—just do your best!

Find the Facts...

1. See if you can state the *content* of this week's passage in a couple of sentences. (Who is speaking, what is taking place, what is the main subject?)

Look for the Heart...

2. What do you think is the main *lesson* of this chapter? (What spiritual truths are taught here? Look for a command, a word of exhortation, a promise, etc.)

Hear Him Speak...

3. Look for a *personal application* from the content of this chapter. It should come from the lesson you got from the chapter (question 2). How will you apply the lesson to yourself?

4. Was there a particular verse that ministered to you this week? What was it and how did it minister to you?

LESSON 2
REVELATION 1:9-20

In the first 8 verses of chapter 1, we looked at the prologue of the Book of Revelation. We learned that this book is the revelation of Jesus Christ—*the exalted and risen King of kings and Lord of lords!* In this book, then, we will *see Jesus*. We learned that this book was written by the apostle John and that there is a blessing attached to the reading of it. We also learned that it is addressed to the seven churches in Asia, and that, although John penned the book, it is truly from Jesus Christ, *the faithful witness, the first-born of the dead and the ruler of the kings of the earth!* Today we will consider John's vision, specifically what he *heard*, what he *saw*, and his *reaction* to the vision.

Day 1

Read Revelation 1:9-11

What John heard:

1. Although John was the last of the apostles and worthy of high esteem, he reintroduces himself to those who would read this book in two ways: first, as *brother*, second, as *fellow partaker*. What made John their brother?

    a. In what three things was he their *fellow partaker*? v. 9

2. Where was John, according to verse 9? Why?

LESSON 2

   a. How could his very situation relate to his being their fellow partaker in *tribulation*? (Would they have been in tribulation?)

   b. How might you consider yourself a fellow partaker in the *kingdom* with your Christian friend?

   c. Do you see yourself as a fellow partaker in *perseverance* with other Christians? Share your thoughts.

The fact of the matter was that John was exiled to Patmos, a small, rocky, and barren island in the Aegean Sea. He had been sent there by one of the cruelest of Roman Emperors, Domitian, because of his testimony of Christ. As we read the specific letters to the churches we will see that he was not alone in tribulation.

3. In verse 10, John describes the day the vision came. What day of the week was it? Why is it called the Lord's Day?

   a. How does he describe his own state on this particular Lord's Day?

There are some different thoughts on the matter of what John meant by the fact that he was *in the Spirit*. Some think that he was referring to being in a state of worship, meditation, and prayer, remembering His beloved Lord on this the day of His resurrection.

Others think John was referring to the fact that he was supernaturally transported to an experience beyond the normal senses to perceive this revelation from God.

- b. Share from these verses the other times that John mentions being in the Spirit and what he saw:

    ✞ Revelation 4:2

    ✞ Revelation 17:3

    ✞ Revelation 21:10

4. What did John *hear*, and what did it sound like? Revelation 1:10

Throughout Revelation, a loud sound or voice indicates the solemnity of what God is about to reveal. Trumpets are also often spoken of throughout the pages of Scripture as a means of getting the attention of God's people, preceding a word from God, and many times as a warning of what is to come.

- a. Read Joel 2:1. Of what was the trumpet a warning in this verse?

- b. From your basic understanding of the Book of Revelation, could we consider it a warning? Of what is this book a warning? See verse 1 again.

5. Two words of command were given by the voice that sounded like a trumpet:

LESSON 2

✣ What was John to write?

✣ To whom was John to send what he wrote?

We will see more specifically the warning nature of the words spoken to each of the seven churches in the next two chapters.

This week's memory verse:
"'I am the Alpha and the Omega,' says the Lord God, 'Who is and who was and who is to come, the Almighty.'" Revelation 1:8

Day 2

Read Revelation 1:12-16

What John saw:
As we consider the verses at hand today, we will be predominantly looking at the elements of the vision which John had of the risen Christ on this particular Sunday as he worshipped.

1. **Challenge:** Begin today by remembering some of the last times John would have seen Jesus. Share what you can about those moments: what was happening, where was Jesus, where was John, what would Jesus have looked like, etc. (You may see John 1, 20, and Acts 1 for help.)

2. Suddenly there was a loud voice that sounded like a trumpet speaking the word, "Write." John turned around to see who was speaking to him—what did he see? v. 12

a. Verse 20 interprets this symbol for us. What are the seven golden lampstands?

There are actually three ways of looking at the seven churches. The first, of course, is that they were seven actual churches of John's day, the second is that they *represent* seven basic divisions of church history, and the third is that they are *characteristic* of seven types of churches that exist today.

3. How did John describe what he saw in the midst of the lampstands? v. 13a

Son of Man is the title Jesus Christ used most often of Himself during His earthly ministry. John, looking at Jesus at this particular moment, says, He was *like a son of man*. Despite the glory of His appearance, John recognized him to be a man—indeed the very Son of Man. Henry M. Morris calls Him *"the representative man, true man, man as God intended man to be."*

The words *like* and *as* are important in the study of Revelation. They are similes, which are word pictures comparing two things. We will see similes often in our study, indicating that two things are being *compared*. They are not the same but are *like* or *similar* to one another. In today's lesson we will see many such descriptions.

4. Share John's description of the following elements of Jesus' appearance:

   His robe
   His girdle

LESSON 2

His head and hair
His eyes
His feet
His voice

    a. **Challenge**: Consider again the last times John would have seen Jesus and compare the Jesus John had seen on the cross, in the upper room, and on the Mt. of Olives with the Jesus he was seeing now.

John MacArthur says of the vision John had of Christ, *"This vision of Christ is equaled in grandeur only by the vision of His final return as King of kings and Lord of lords."*

    b. See Revelation 19:11-16 for this even more glorious description. Write down what strikes you.

5. Verse 16 continues John's description of the vision of Jesus:

    ✢ What was in Jesus' right hand (v. 16)? How does verse 20 interpret this symbol?

    ✢ What was in Jesus' mouth? What does Ephesians 6:17 interpret this symbol to be? What does Hebrews 4:12 add to these thoughts?

✣ How does John describe His face (v. 16b)?

Only on the Mount of Transfiguration had John seen Jesus thus appear (Matthew 17:1-2). There was no doubt about it—this was indeed *Jesus Christ, the divine Son of God!*

Review this week's memory verse.

Day 3

Read Revelation 1:17-20

What John did:
1. What did John do as a result of the vision of Christ?

We know that John had once been very familiar with Jesus, in fact he called himself, *"the one Jesus loved."* In John 13:23, we see him lay his head on His very breast. And yet now, his reaction is quite different.

    a. How does 2 Corinthians 5:16b help us to understand the difference?

2. Jesus speaks immediate words of comfort: *"Do not be afraid."* And then proceeds to give John three reasons why he need not be:

    ✣ *I Am*
    ✣ *I Am*
    ✣ *I Am*

LESSON 2

The first *I am* speaks of Christ's eternal nature; the second *I am* speaks of Christ's sacrificial death and resurrection; the third *I am* speaks of the fact that He will never die again and therefore will always be.

   a. How do the final words of Jesus, as recorded in Matthew 28:20, give us a comforting sense of these facts?

It's interesting to note that the first *"Fear not"* of the Bible occurs just before the first *"I Am."*

   b. From each of these *I Ams,* can you share why *you* need not be afraid?

3. Following the three *I Ams* in Revelation 1:17-18, Jesus gives one more reason John need not fear: *"I have …"* What does Jesus have? (v. 18b)

   a. Why do you think this is significant? You might see Hebrews 2:14-15 for help. How could this realization help *you* not to be afraid? (You may also see 1 Corinthians 15:55-57.)

Henry Morris says, *"Multitudes of religious philosophers have searched for the key to life and death, but Christ claims to have the key."* Warren Wiersbe says this: *"The One with the keys is the One who has authority."*

It is said that Revelation is the only book of the Bible that has an inspired outline of its contents. Jesus Christ gives us the outline as He says, *"Write therefore:"*

- *"The things which you have seen,"* speaking of John's vision in chapter 1
- *"The things which are,"* referring to the letters to the 7 churches—chapters 2-3
- *"The things which shall take place after these things,"* speaking of the revelation of future events given in chapters 4-22

In verse 20, Jesus explains two mysteries which we have already seen, the mystery of the seven stars and the mystery of the seven golden lampstands. Henry Morris says that most often in the book of Revelation when symbols are used they are explained internally. This is a case in point.

4. What, again, according to verse 20 are the seven stars which Jesus holds in His right hand?

There is much debate over whether these angels are actual angels or if they are really the pastors or elders over the seven churches. The word translated angel has the basic meaning of messenger. This is why many modern expositors have deduced that Jesus was actually speaking of the leaders of these churches.

However, there is another point of view. Because Henry Morris believes in the principle of natural, literal interpretation, and the fact that this particular word is translated 67 other times in this book to mean *angel*, he holds to the fact that Jesus is indeed speaking of angels here and understands this to mean that all true churches of the Lord have angels assigned to their care.

a. Hebrews 1:14 gives a description of the ministry of angels. What do we learn about them there?

b. What further sense of the ministry of angels is found in Matthew 18:10?

5. What, again, are the 7 golden lampstands?

a. **Challenge**: Why do you think the lampstand is a fitting symbol for the church? Can you personalize this?

Review this week's memory verse.

Day 4

Overview of Revelation 1:9-20

In this section we will be looking at the passage we have studied this week as a whole. The goal is to find the main lessons the Lord has for us from this chapter. Don't worry about being clever or profound—just do your best!

Find the Facts ...

1. See if you can state the *content* of this week's passage in a couple of sentences. (Who is speaking, what is taking place, what is the main subject?)

Look for the Heart....

2. What do you think is the main *lesson* of this chapter? (What spiritual truths are taught here? Look for a command, a word of exhortation, a promise, etc.)

Hear Him Speak...

3. Look for a *personal application* from the content of this chapter. It should come from the lesson you got from the chapter (question 2). How will you apply the lesson to yourself?

4. Was there a particular verse that ministered to you this week? What was it and how did it minister to you?

LESSON 3
REVELATION 2:1-7

Here we begin the letters to the seven churches: Christ's message to His body. In this lesson, we will look at the letter to Ephesus. The letters are interesting in that they have a pattern. Each one begins with a characteristic of Christ taken from His description in Revelation 1. Next, Christ commends His church—each church receiving a commendation, except Laodicea. Following the commendation, Christ then rebukes His church for their errors. Only two churches—Smyrna and Philadelphia—receive no rebuke. Next, Christ exhorts each church and finally leaves them with a promise. Remember as you study the letters to the churches that, although they were written to actual churches of John's day, they have an individual message to the believer today. See where you stand in relation to Christ's word to His Church—if you need to make corrections, then make them—the time draws nigh: *"Blessed is he who reads and those who hear the words of the prophecy, and heed the things which are written in it; for the time is near."* Revelation 1:3

Day 1

Read Revelation 2:1-4

To the angel of the church in Ephesus write:
1. How does Christ describe Himself to the church at Ephesus? v. 1 Look back and see where this description is found in chapter 1.

a. What did chapter 1 tell us was the meaning of the seven golden lampstands and the seven stars?

As a *city*, Ephesus was the largest city of the province of Asia and considered the *Vanity Fair* of the ancient world. It was an important city commercially, politically, and religiously; the location of the great temple of Artemis (Diana), one of the seven wonders of the world. As a *church*, Ephesus was extremely important—in fact, the most prominent in the area, actually the mother of the Asian churches. Paul established Christianity in Ephesus, spending three years there. After Paul, Timothy ministered at Ephesus, and John spent his old age there.

It is to Ephesus that Jesus says: *"The one who holds the seven stars in His right hand (the hand of power) and walks among the seven golden lampstands, says this ..."*

2. State the points of Christ's commendation of the Ephesian church found in verses 2-3.

William Barclay says that when Christ speaks of the Ephesians' *deeds* (works, KJV) He is actually referring to those works being their *toil* and *perseverance* (labor and patience, KJV). The Greek word for labor is *kopos*, which means *the toil which exhausts,* and the Greek word for patience is *hupomone*, which would better be translated *triumphant fortitude*.

a. Does it encourage you to know that Jesus—the one who walks among the churches *sees* and *knows* all that you do in His name? Could it be said of you that you work the works of the Ephesian church?

LESSON 3

✣ *How are you "working"—could your service be called sacrificial? See John 9:4*

✣ *Are you persevering, or is your faith less than triumphant? Have you grown weary? See 1 Corinthians 15:58*

✣ *Do you put your teachers to the test—rejecting any teaching that is not according to Scripture? See Acts 17:11*

3. What did Jesus have against this church? v. 4

It's interesting to note that this church, which had such a high level of *service,* was lacking in devotion to Christ.

   a. Do you believe that you can serve the Lord without being devoted to Him? Have you done this? Are you doing this now?

   b. How did Paul describe this kind of service in 1 Corinthians 13:1-3. Share your thoughts on this.

This week's memory verse:
"He who has an ear, let him hear what the Spirit says to the churches." Revelation 2:7a

Day 2

Read Revelation 2:4-7

Although a long list of commendation and approval is given for the works of the church of Ephesus, Christ has one word of accusation, and a serious one at that. This hard-working church had left their first love. They were indeed still working, but their motivation was no longer fervent love for their Savior. To the world, this church would have looked perfect—only Christ could see the truth.

1. See if you can describe a first-love experience from the relationship of a husband and wife. If you are married, you may remember how you felt and what you did in response to those first love feelings—if not, how you imagine it would be.

    a. Now, describe the first love experience of a new believer in Christ. Remember how it was for you? Write down some of what you remember of the early days of your relationship with your Savior.

2. Ezekiel 16:8-14 gives us a beautiful portrayal of God taking Jerusalem as His bride. Share briefly what stands out to you of the beauty of this relationship.

a. In Jeremiah 2:2, God remembers this time. What does He say?

Sadly, Ezekiel 16:15-34 goes on to reveal the lack of love of Jerusalem for her husband, the Lord God. Verse 22 says, *"And besides all your abominations and harlotries* **you did not remember the days of your youth** *..."* God remembered (Jeremiah 2:2), but Jerusalem did not.

3. Something to think about:

✝ Consider how a husband must feel when he realizes his wife no longer adores him but is only going through the motions.

✝ Consider how God must have felt when Jerusalem, His beloved, turned from His love, worshipped other gods, and forgot from whence they came.

✝ Consider how Christ must have felt when He saw the church of Ephesus doing what appeared to be good works *for Him*, but discerned that in reality they had lost their love for *Him, the one who had saved them.*

✝ Share any thoughts you have ...

4. Christ's exhortation to Ephesus has three parts: *remember, repent* and *do*. v. 5

a. What were they to remember? Do you need to remember this? You have already shared how it was for you as a new believer—are you still there? Share your thoughts.

The Amplified Bible translates verse 5 this way: *"Remember then from what heights you have fallen ..."* If you have left your first love, then you are in a much lower place than Christ intends you to be. If you are serving Him without really loving Him, then the quality of your service is questionable at best, and your rewards will be like the wood, hay, and straw spoken of in 1 Corinthians 3:12-15.

5. Christ's command to them was *repent*. The word repent means not only to be sorry for our sin but to turn from it—to change our direction. How were they to do this? (v. 5)

    a. What are some things **you** might do to follow this command? (What are some of the things you did at first?)

    b. Why would doing the deeds you did at first renew your love relationship with the Lord?

6. What would happen if this church didn't respond to Christ's exhortation? v. 5

William Barclay makes note that, *"The church which has ceased to shine for Christ has lost the reason for its existence."* And *Halley's Bible Handbook*, speaking of the warning that their candlestick would be removed says, *"It has. The site of Ephesus is deserted."*

    a. What promise was made to the one who would overcome? v. 7

    b. Look at Revelation 22:1-5 for a description of this *Paradise of God*. What most blesses you as you read these words?

Although the warning to the Ephesian church as a whole seems to have gone unheeded, this promise is to the individual: the individual who *overcomes*. Are you an *overcomer*?

Review this week's memory verse.

Day 3: Worshipping the Lord

Read Revelation 4:4-11

In this section, beginning with this lesson, we will take the opportunity to look at some of the things which are particular to the Book of Revelation. We will look at such things as the *Keys to Revelation*, the significance of the number 7 in this book, as well as other exciting subjects. In this lesson, we will see the important part worship plays in this unique and exciting book!

1. In each of the following verses, we will witness the worship of the Lord. Answer the following questions for each passage—and be sure to look for the unique aspects of worship in each case:

Revelation 4:8
- ✞ Who is worshipping the Lord?
- ✞ How, specifically, are they worshipping Him?

Revelation 4:10-11
- ✞ Who is worshipping the Lord?
- ✞ How, specifically, are they worshipping Him?

Revelation 5:11-12
- ✞ Who is worshipping the Lord?
- ✞ How, specifically, are they worshipping Him?

Revelation 5:13
- ✞ Who is worshipping the Lord?
- ✞ How, specifically, are they worshipping Him?

Revelation 7:9-10
- ✞ Who is worshipping the Lord?
- ✞ How, specifically, are they worshipping Him?

LESSON 3

Revelation 7:11-12
- ✢ *Who is worshipping the Lord?*
- ✢ *How, specifically, are they worshipping Him?*

Revelation 19:1-3
- ✢ *Who is worshipping the Lord?*
- ✢ *How, specifically, are they worshipping Him?*

Revelation 19:4-5
- ✢ *Who is worshipping the Lord?*
- ✢ *How, specifically, are they worshipping Him?*

Revelation 19:6-7
- ✢ *Who is worshipping the Lord?*
- ✢ *How, specifically, are they worshipping Him?*

In all, there are actually 14 doxologies of praise and worship recorded in the Book of Revelation. Each one is spoken by different beings, some spoken in particular to God the Father, some to the Lamb (Christ), and some to both God the Father and the Lamb. The number 14 is significant to the Book of Revelation, as it is a multiple of the number 7. We will look into this in the future.

2. From this small glimpse of heaven, what is revealed to you about your future there?

    a. How do we get a sense of this in Philippians 2:9-11?

3. In our verses today, we have seen Jesus **worshipped**. Do you understand the difference between worship and thanksgiving? Go back and look at some of the examples of worship given here and share your thoughts.

4. Why is Jesus worthy of our worship?

    a. Write a song of worship to your Savior of about two or three sentences.

See if you can spend the first five minutes of your prayer time this week *just in worship*—no requests, thanksgiving, or confession. This is not necessarily an easy thing to do, but as with anything, practice makes perfect! Follow your time of worship with *confession, thanksgiving,* and *supplications.* This formula for prayer is known as:

LESSON 3

***A**—Adoration*
***C**—Confession*
***T**—Thanksgiving*
***S**—Supplication*

It is a good pattern to follow in your prayers from now on!

Review this week's memory verse.

Day 4

Overview of Revelation 2:1-7

In this section we will be looking at the passage we have studied this week as a whole. The goal is to find the main lessons the Lord has for us from this chapter. Don't worry about being clever or profound—just do your best!

Find the Facts...

1. See if you can state the *content* of this week's passage in a couple of sentences. (Who is speaking, what is taking place, what is the main subject?)

Look for the Heart...

2. What do you think is the main *lesson* of this chapter? (What spiritual truths are taught here? Look for a command, a word of exhortation, a promise, etc.)

Hear Him Speak ...

3. Look for a *personal application* from the content of this chapter. It should come from the lesson you got from the chapter (question 2). How will you apply the lesson to yourself?

4. Was there a particular verse that ministered to you this week? What was it and how did it minister to you?

LESSON 4
REVELATION 2:8-11

Smyrna was a great city, outstandingly beautiful, and extremely proud: it claimed to be the *Glory of Asia*. It also claimed to be first in Caesar worship. Under the reign of Domitian, the worship of Caesar became compulsory. Each citizen had to burn a pinch of incense on the altar to the godhead of Caesar, at which time a certificate was given to guarantee this had been done. Not to make this sacrifice to Caesar branded a person disloyal and made him an outlaw. The Christians, then, who refused to worship any but God, were under constant threat of persecution. It has been said that *nowhere can life have been more dangerous for a Christian than in Smyrna.*

Day 1

Read Revelation 2:8-9

And to the angel of the church in Smyrna write:

1. With what words did Jesus describe Himself to the church of Smyrna? v. 8 Look back and see where this description is found in chapter 1.

2. Just as Jesus knew the Ephesians, He also knew the people of Smyrna. What did He know about them? v. 9

The word used for tribulation in verse 9 is the Greek word *thlipsis*, which means *pressure*. The word used for poverty—*ptocheia*—speaks of *destitution*. It describes the one who has nothing at all.

It is thought that the Jews who were blaspheming these Christians were as those Judaizers who followed Paul throughout his journeys, trying to dilute grace with legalism and ceremonialism, both of which are sub-Christian—*religion* at best—and anti-Christ. Therefore, they are called a synagogue of Satan.

    a. Although Jesus said that He knew of their poverty, what did He say was really the case? v. 9

    b. Contrast this with His words to the Laodicean church in Revelation 3:17.

    c. Explain the difference in these two churches in regard to wealth: who was in the better position, in reality? What does 2 Corinthians 4:18 teach us about this?

Something to think about: Are you wealthy in earthly possessions, or are your possessions spiritual and eternal in nature?

3. Consider Jesus' word to this church in verse 10:

    ✝ What was going to happen to them?

    ✝ What were they to do?

LESSON 4

✞ What would they receive?

Future suffering for this church was certain. But the exhortation to them was: *"Do not fear ... be faithful until death."*

4. Hebrews 11:32-40 speaks of the persecution of God's people over the years. From this passage, name some of the types of persecution that may have been faced by the early church.

    a. According to these verses, how did they *gain their approval?*

5. Do you think it's possible that you, too, will suffer persecution as a Christian? See 2 Timothy 3:12

    a. What are you to do in that case?

The name *Smyrna* means *myrrh.* An interesting fact about myrrh is that *it must be crushed to give forth its fragrance ...*

This week's memory verse:
"For momentary, light affliction is producing for us an eternal weight of glory far beyond all comparison." 2 Corinthians 4:17

Day 2

Read Revelation 2:10-11

For the second time in Revelation we read the words, *"Do not fear."* The Amplified says, *"Fear nothing that you are about to suffer. Dismiss your dread and fears!"* This is something easier said than done! Not just anyone can tell you with authority not to be afraid. It would depend on who is speaking whether or not you can take the words to heart.

1. Who is speaking to the believers in Smyrna? (Notice how He identifies Himself in verse 8.)

   a. Did He understand their situation? (v. 9) Did He know what their future held? (v. 10) How would these facts help them to take heed and to *"fear not what they were about to suffer"*?

2. We may not live in the identical situation as the believers in Smyrna, but we do live in a dark and changing world. Would it help you to know that the Lord has spoken these same words to you? He has! The Word of God is full of exhortations to *"fear not."* Look up these wonderful verses and share what you glean from them:

   Deuteronomy 31:6, 8

   Isaiah 41:10

   Isaiah 43:1

Luke 12:7

Luke 12:32

3. Not only are we told to *fear not,* but we can exclaim, *I will not fear!* From the following Psalms, why can we say we will not fear?

    23:4

    27:1

    46:1

    118:6

God's words to Joshua say it well: *"Have I not commanded you? Be strong and courageous! Do not tremble or be dismayed, for the Lord your God is with you wherever you go"* (Joshua 1:9).

4. The Savior makes two *promises* to His church at Smyrna. What is *promised*:

    ✝ *To the one who is faithful unto death?* v. 10

    a. What does James tell us about the crown of life in James 1:12?

There are many crowns promised to those who belong to Christ. You may look at the following verses which speak of our crowns: 1 Corinthians 9:25; 1 Thessalonians 2:19; 2 Timothy 4:6-8; James 1:12; 1 Peter 5:4. *Which of these will you be receiving?*

✝ *To the one who overcomes?* v. 11

b. Read Revelation 20:11-15 and 21:8 and see if you can explain what the second death is.

There is a bumper sticker that reads: *Born once, die twice; born twice, die once.* How many times have you been born? *"Truly, truly, I say to you, unless one is born again, he cannot see the kingdom of God."* John 3:3

5. Considering what we have learned about the church at Smyrna, read Romans 8:35-37 and answer these questions:

   ✝ *Why were the Smyrnians able to have hope in spite of the promise of future suffering?*

   ✝ *Why are **you** able to have hope in spite of the circumstances you are facing? (Take this to heart and share your thoughts in a personal way.)*

One of the most famous martyrdoms in history was that of Polycarp, Bishop of Smyrna. At the point of being put to death he said, *"I fear not the fire that burns for a season and after a while is quenched ..."* and as the flames licked his body he prayed his great prayer: *"I thank Thee that Thou hast graciously thought me worthy of this day and of this hour, that I may receive a portion in the number of the martyrs, in the cup of Thy Christ."*

One last fact to consider about Smyrna in contrast to Ephesus: though Ephesus is now gone (remember the words of Christ that unless they repented He would remove their lampstand out of its place), Smyrna still stands strong, a city of 250,000 inhabitants.

Review this week's memory verse.

Day 3: Keys to Revelation

Today we are going to consider the important *keys* of this exciting apocalyptic book.

In the first place, let's look at the name of this book. In the Greek it is actually titled *Apokalypsis Ioannou*, "Revelation of John." A more accurate title comes from the first verse, *Apokalypsis Iesou Christoue*, "Revelation of Jesus Christ."

This title, **"Revelation of Jesus Christ,"** is the **key word** of the book.

The word *apocalypse* means unveiling or disclosure, and it tells us that this book is *an unveiling of that which otherwise could not be known.* Through our study of Revelation, we will see unveiled the divine character of God and His program of redemption as brought to completion through His Son Jesus Christ.

1. The first **key verse** to the Book of Revelation is actually the verse that gives an outline of the book as a whole. Only in this book of the Bible is the outline given in its contents! Look up Revelation 1:19 and write out the key verse in outline form.

    "Write therefore:"
    - ✞
    - ✞
    - ✞

These words were, of course, spoken to John. ***The things which you have seen*** refers to the vision given to John at this time. ***The things which are*** speak of the messages to the seven churches of John's day, ***the things which shall take place after these things*** refers to the entire rest of the book of Revelation, beginning in chapter 4.

   a. Look at Revelation 4:1 for the words that begin the third division of this book. What exciting words these are! Notice in Revelation 1:19, the third part of the outline reads: *"The things which shall take place **after these things**."* With what words does Revelation 4:1 begin?

2. The second **key verse** in Revelation is actually a group of verses: Revelation 19:11-16. Read these verses and answer the following questions:

   a. Of whom is this passage speaking?

   b. Describe Him from this passage. (Do you notice how many characteristics of His description in this passage are ones which we have already seen in our study of Revelation?)

   c. In this passage, He is called three names. After each name, share either your understanding of its truth or your personal joy at that aspect of your Savior's character and position.

   Verse 11

LESSON 4

   Verse 13

   Verse 16

3. **Challenge**: See if you understand the importance of this group of verses. What is actually happening here?

4. The **key chapters** in the Book of Revelation are chapters 19-22. Read these four incredible chapters for God's plan for the last days and for all of eternity. Share at least three highlights for you personally from the contents of these chapters.

   1.

   2.

   3.

5. Another very important verse in Revelation is 1:3.

   a. In a word, what is the promise of this verse?

   b. To whom is it promised?

   c. What information is given as to the time factor for these things?

6. As we read and study the Book of Revelation, and as we live our lives during this the final chapter in the history of the world, what promise of Jesus from the final chapter in this book should we hold firm in our hearts? Revelation 22:20

a. How will this make a difference in the way you live?

Review this week's memory verse.

Day 4

Overview of Revelation 2:8-11

In this section we will be looking at the passage we have studied this week as a whole. The goal is to find the main lessons the Lord has for us from this chapter. Don't worry about being clever or profound—just do your best!

Find the Facts ...

1. See if you can state the *content* of this week's passage in a couple of sentences. (Who is speaking, what is taking place, what is the main subject?)

Look for the Heart ...

What do you think is the main *lesson* of this chapter? (What spiritual truths are taught here? Look for a command, a word of exhortation, a promise, etc.)

Hear Him Speak ...

3. Look for a *personal application* from the content of this chapter. It should come from the lesson you got from the chapter (question 2). How will you apply the lesson to yourself?

4. Was there a particular verse that ministered to you this week? What was it and how did it minister to you?

LESSON 5
REVELATION 2:12-17

The heart of the message to the next two churches we will look at—Pergamum and Thyatira—seems to have to do with *compromise* and *tolerance*. In a world where tolerance seems to have become the new byword—with only *intolerance* not being tolerated, we would do well to *"hear what the Spirit says to the churches."*

The city of Pergamum, situated 60 miles north of Smyrna, was the capital and, historically, the greatest city in Asia Minor. It was a place known for its learning, refinement, and science—especially medicine—one of its two most prominent religious systems being the worship of Asclepius, the god of healing. Just as Ephesus was the church of departed love and Smyrna the church of persecution, Pergamum was the church of worldly alliance—the word Pergamum meaning *marriage.* It was in this church age that the emperor Constantine declared Christianity the official religion of Rome. Rather than being a good thing, it has been seen through history that this was in fact a tool of Satan who could not destroy the church through persecution and so, instead, weakened it through compromise and indulgence.

Day 1
Read Revelation 2:12-13

And to the angel of the church in Pergamum write:
1. How does Christ describe Himself to the church in Pergamum? v. 12 Look back and see where this description is found in chapter 1.

a. What do we understand to be the significance of the sharp two-edged sword? Ephesians 6:17

b. What is this *sword of the Spirit* able to do? Hebrews 4:12

2. Who is the Word of God? John 1:1, 14

    a. What does John 14:6 reveal to us about Jesus Christ?

3. Twice in verse 13 we are given insight into the spiritual state of the city of Pergamum. Whose dwelling place is it according to this verse?

Henry Morris says "Pergamos (Pergamum) had become probably the greatest center of pagan religion in the world at that time." And, referring to Alexander Hislop's famous book *Two Babylons,* indicates that "Pergamos had inherited the religious mantle of ancient Babylon when Babylon fell in the days of Belshazzar." Tim LaHaye agrees with this thought and says that when Babylon's glory began to decline, "Satan looked for another location. He selected Pergamum because of its strong idolatrous religions." Later, his throne would move to Rome. Is it possible that it is now situated here in America?

    a. Jesus was not unaware of the conditions of this church. How (again) does He indicate this in verse 13a?

    b. What two words of commendation did He have for this church? (v.13)

It is not known for certain exactly who Antipas of verse 13 is, but it is thought that he was a local Christian in Pergamum who sealed the testimony of his faith with his blood.

    c. How does the martyrdom of Antipas reveal the significance of the faithfulness of the rest of the church at Pergamum?

    d. Is there a condition in your life or surroundings that makes it difficult for you to hold fast to Christ's name? Does it help you to know that *He knows where you dwell*? What comfort does Isaiah 49:16 give you?

Although this church was commended for remaining faithful and holding fast to Christ's name, there were serious problems in the church; namely, the infiltration of false teaching: the teaching of Balaam to eat things sacrificed to idols and to commit acts of immorality, and the teaching of the Nicolaitans. It is not completely clear what the teaching of the Nicolaitans was, but it was most certainly a dangerous false teaching and was hated by Christ (Revelation 2:6).

We will look at the significance of Jesus' reference to the teachings of Balaam in the next day's study.

This week's memory verse:
"Sanctify them in the truth; Thy word is truth." John 17:17

LESSON 5

Day 2
Read Revelation 2:14-17

To understand the reference to Balaam, we must look to the book of Numbers (22-24) where we learn that Balaam was a false prophet who was hired by Balak, king of Moab, to bring a curse upon Israel. Unable to bring forth a curse but only blessing, Balaam, it seems, instructed Balak to cast a stumbling block at Israel. (See Numbers 31:16.)

1. Read Numbers 25:1-5. Verse 2 reveals the stumbling block (according to the counsel of Balaam). What did the Moabites do to the Israelites?

    a. What did the Israelites do?

    verse 1b
    verse 3

    b. Verse 4 reveals the severity of this sin. What did God do?

2. Read 2 Corinthians 6:14-18. What do you learn there?

    a. What kinds of relationships with unbelievers do you think it is speaking of here? v. 14a

3. **Challenge**: Why would it be so harmful for Israel to be united with Moab? (There are many reasons.)

a. Why is it harmful for you to be united with unbelievers? (This passage speaks of being *bound together,* not simply knowing or having casual relationships with unbelievers.)

b. How is your being *bound together* with unbelievers a compromise to your Christianity?

c. **Personal**: Are there any relationships in your life that fall into this category? What does 2 Corinthians 6:17 command?

d. What is promised to the one who *comes out from their midst and is separate?* v. 18

4. What was Jesus' word to the ones in Pergamum who taught and lived this way? Revelation 2:16

This is a basic principle of God: *Repent or be judged by the Word.* John 17:17 says, *"Thy Word is truth."*

a. How can we keep from being judged by the Word? 1 Corinthians 11:31a

b. What do you think this means?

LESSON 5

5. What is promised to the one who overcomes? Revelation 2:17

The hidden manna speaks of spiritual provision. The white stone possibly refers to the fact that in ancient times in a court trial a white stone signified acquittal. Another possibility is the fact that a white stone was used as a ticket to enter a feast. Each of these thoughts gives us the sense that aligning ourselves by compromise with the world will only bring judgment, while aligning ourselves with Jesus will result in all spiritual provision and blessing. *"Come you who are blessed of My Father, inherit the kingdom prepared for you from the foundation of the world."* Matthew 25:34

   a. Isaiah 62 speaks about our new name—as well as our new state. Read verses 2-5 and share the verse which most encourages and inspires you.

Review this week's memory verse.

Day 3: Genesis and Revelation

The relationship between the Books of Genesis and Revelation is fascinating. *"Just as Genesis is the book of beginnings, Revelation is the book of consummation. In it, the divine program of redemption is brought to fruition, and the holy name of God is vindicated before all creation"* (Bruce Wilkinson). The Book of Genesis records the real events of earth's primeval ages; the Book of Revelation describes the real events of the ages to come. Genesis means *"beginnings;"* Revelation means *"unveiling"* of something previously concealed.

REVELATION

In comparing the first three chapters of the Bible with the last three chapters we discover some wonderful things—the contrast being between the temporal and the eternal and the cursed and the redeemed. You may wish to scan these chapters before you begin this lesson. This entire day of study will be a challenge.

✟ **Challenge**: Put a marker in Genesis 1 and in Revelation 20, as we will be comparing these two passages of Scripture. See if you can discover in the following verses the contrast between what took place as recorded in Genesis and what will take place as recorded in Revelation. Share in a few words what you discover. You will have to think! Just do your best.

Genesis 1-3	*Revelation 20-22*
1:1:	21:1:
1:5:	21:25:
1:16:	21:23:
2:17:	21:4:
3:1:	20:10:
3:6-7:	21:27:
3:8-10:	21:3:
3:13:	20:10; 22:3:
3:16:	21:4:
3:17:	22:3:

LESSON 5

3:19:   22:5:

3:23:   21:25:

3:24:   22:14:

3:24:   22:4:

Bruce Wilkinson says of Revelation: *"In a very real sense, chapters 21-22 are the new Genesis, but this time there will be no fall. In broadest terms, the Bible gives the story of God's work in creation, redemption and re-creation, and it centers on the incarnation of the God-man."*

The amazing and most encouraging words of the Bible are found in the final verses, *"He who testifies to these things says, 'Yes, I am coming quickly.'"* To which we reply, *"Amen. Come Lord Jesus."* Revelation 22:20

Review this week's memory verse.

Day 4

Overview of Revelation 2:12-17

In this section we will be looking at the passage we have studied this week as a whole. The goal is to find the main lessons the Lord has for us from this chapter. Don't worry about being clever or profound—just do your best!

Find the Facts ...

1. See if you can state the *content* of this week's passage in a couple of sentences. (Who is speaking, what is taking place, what is the main subject?)

Look for the Heart...

2. What do you think is the main *lesson* of this chapter? (What spiritual truths are taught here? Look for a command, a word of exhortation, a promise, etc.)

Hear Him Speak...

3. Look for a *personal application* from the content of this chapter. It should come from the lesson you got from the chapter (question 2). How will you apply the lesson to yourself?

4. Was there a particular verse that ministered to you this week? What was it and how did it minister to you?

LESSON 6
REVELATION 2:18-29

Thyatira was the smallest of the seven cities and, in contrast, rather unimportant. Unlike Ephesus, Smyrna, and Pergamum, it didn't boast great things. One thing it did boast was an important trade center. In fact, it was from Thyatira that Paul's first convert in Europe, Lydia, came. You may remember that she was a seller of purple. That was this city's claim to fame—its wool trade and dyeing industry. Because of this, Thyatira possessed more trade guilds than any other town its size in Asia. This was actually what caused Thyatira its greatest problem. The trade guilds were much like unions. If you didn't belong to one, you would not be able to work at your trade. For the Christian, this was a crucial point, because mixed in with the trade guild meetings was idol worship and immorality.

Day 1

Read Revelation 2:18-29 (concentrating on verses 18-20)

And to the angel of the church in Thyatira write:

1. With what words did Jesus describe Himself to the church in Thyatira? v. 18 Look back and see where this description is found in chapter 1.

    a. List the six words of commendation spoken to the Thyatirans in verse 19.

This list looks very commendable, and in fact in itself it was. Thyatira was the opposite of Ephesus in that its later works were greater than the first. But these are works, and as important as our works can be, they do not compensate for a lack of truth. As Warren Wiersbe says, *"No amount of works can compensate for tolerance of evil."* Thyatira tolerated evil and false teaching. It was a compromising church, and it was a corrupt church. As we begin our thoughts today, you may wish to examine yourself: are you tolerant of that which God hates? His Word is truth. It reveals what is true and what is false. Do you live according to the Word of God, or are you compromising by being tolerant of that which the world calls good. Have you joined yourself to the world, or are you separated from the world? Compromise leads to corruption, in a church and in a life.

2. What was Christ's complaint with the church at Thyatira? v. 20 What was Jezebel teaching this church?

   a. See Revelation 2:14. What were the things being taught to the church in Pergamum?

   b. Read Acts 15:19-20, where the council in Jerusalem came to a decision of what would be required of Gentile converts to Christianity. What were those requirements? v.20

In the Ten Commandments, the issue of sexual immorality is defined in the commandment which says, *"You shall not commit adultery."* Of course we know that sexual immorality covers more ground than this—it speaks of *any* sexual activity outside the bonds of marriage.

We have already noted that the trade guild meetings often degenerated into affairs of drunkenness and immorality. But even more damaging to the believer was the worship of idols.

    c. Read the first 6 verses of Exodus 20. What is at the heart of these first two commandments?

The believers in Thyatira may not have been actually making idols and worshipping them, but by being part of the trade guilds—the only way in which they could get work—and participating in their meetings, they would indirectly be worshipping idols. The meal would begin and end with a cup of wine poured out as an offering to the pagan gods. The meal itself would almost always follow a sacrifice, a part of the animal being offered on the altar to the pagan god. To take part in the meal would be taking part in idol worship. Jezebel, it seems, encouraged the people at Thyatira that this was not wrong.

3. When something is clearly against God's revealed will and not going along with it will result in hardship (the loss of a job or a promotion, the loss of a relationship, etc.) a choice has to be made: to obey God or to compromise. In order not to take part in this form of idolatry and to obey God by worshipping Him alone, what would the believer in Thyatira have had to do?

Have you ever had to make a difficult choice along this same line? (If you have walked with God for any length of time you have probably had to make several!)

a. Share a time when you chose the blessing of God, though it meant certain sacrifice, over the promise the world offered for your compromise. Or, share your experience of making the *wrong* choice at a crucial moment—sometimes our failure becomes our greatest teacher.

b. Who would the believer in Thyatira have to trust in order to do what was right? Who do you need to trust when you are up against such a difficult circumstance? What promise does Philippians 4:19 give to the one who trusts in God?

c. Write out the word of promise to the uncompromising believer found in Isaiah 64:4.

This week's memory verse:
"Test all things; hold fast what is good." 1Thessalonians 5:21

Day 2

Read Revelation 2:20-29

The very way Jesus Christ describes Himself to the church in Thyatira gives evidence of the fact that the letter is a severe warning of judgment to come. The great problem of this church being its tolerance for the teaching of the woman called Jezebel. It is most unlikely that this woman's name was actually Jezebel, more likely she was given the name because of her likeness to the wicked Jezebel of the Old Testament—the wife of the most evil King Ahab—who brought the worship of Baal into Israel, thereby defiling the worship of the one true God.

LESSON 6

The Bible is full of strong warnings about those who would teach us false doctrine. It seems that this "Jezebel" was a woman of considerable importance and powerful influence who allowed and perhaps even argued that the church be permitted to compromise with the world. In his book, *Letters to the Seven Churches,* William Barclay shows how very critical this problem was for the church: *"Beyond a doubt compromise would have meant absorption in heathenism; the continued existence of the church depended on the continued determination of the church to be different from the world."*

1. Looking back at verse 20, although Jezebel is the one who is bringing in the false teaching, what again does Jesus have against *the church?*

    a. Notice in verses 22 and 23, who is to be judged along with *Jezebel.*

2. 1 John 4:1 reveals our personal responsibility in the matter of discerning between false and true teaching. (You may want to read this whole passage—verses 1-6.) What does verse 1 tell us to do?

    a. 1 John 4:5 defines the teacher and teaching that is to be rejected. What does it say?

    b. The Bereans are a great example to us in this. What practical thing did they do with what they were taught? Acts 17:11

These Scriptures reveal the importance of our Bible study and our daily Bible reading. We should also pray and ask God to give us the gift of discerning spirits (1 Corinthians 12:10) that we might be able to distinguish between a true and a false teacher. From what we read here in Revelation 2, we see that *we* are responsible for what we hear, what we take in, and what we continue to take in.

    c. What does Titus 3:9-11 command us to do when we recognize we are being led astray?

It's interesting that verse 10 speaks of a first and second warning. The false teacher, then, is to be given an opportunity to repent. Revelation 2:21 reveals that Jezebel was given that opportunity but did not avail herself of it. This verse gives example of the Lord's grace and longsuffering. When both the false prophetess and her followers rejected it, only judgment remained.

3. Read the promise of judgment upon Jezebel and her followers in verses 21-23:

    a. What would the churches understand when they saw this come to pass? (v. 23)

    b. How is this a promise of good to those who truly obey God?

4. What was the word to those who were **not** holding to the teaching of Jezebel? vv.24-25

These are those who already judged the situation and rejected the teaching of this wicked woman. To them Jesus says, *"I place no other burden on you"*—they had already fulfilled their personal responsibility to *test the spirits*. Remember again, this was a church that was given undiluted praise for their deeds, faith, love, service, and perseverance. The only thing He asked was that they hold fast in their resistance to evil until He came.

5. What was promised to those who overcame? vv. 26-28

These who had to sacrifice in this world, in order not to partake of its sin, would one day rule over it!

   a. Who is the *morning star* that the overcomer is promised? See 2 Peter 1:19 and Revelation 22:16

Review this week's memory verse.

Day 3: Angels in Revelation

People have always had a fascination with angels—especially in our day and age. In fact, over the last few years angels have been given a place of prominence in a sort of New Age spirituality where people believe in angels who don't believe in Jesus. In essence, they have been made to be idols: a safe way to be spiritual and to worship without being hampered by the truth of God's Word. But this new awareness of angels is not in accordance with truth and certainly not in accordance with the wishes of the angels themselves. Today, we will look at angels from the perspective of who they really are, why they were created, and the part they play in the Book of Revelation.

1. The following Scriptures give us some insight into angels. Share briefly from each verse or group of verses what you gather as it applies to the heading:

   ✞ Angels are created beings:
   Colossians 1:16

   ✞ They are organized and ranked:
   Isaiah 6:1-3
   Daniel 10:13
   Ephesians 3:10
   Jude 9

   ✞ Angels were created to serve God:
   Psalm 103:20

   ✞ How they ministered to Jesus:
   Matthew 2:13
   Matthew 4:11
   Matthew 28:2
   Luke 22:43

   ✞ How they minister to us:
   Matthew 18:10
   Hebrews 1:14

   ✞ How many angels are there?
   Hebrews 12:22
   Revelation 5:11

   ✞ Are we to worship angels?
   Colossians 2:18
   Revelation 22:8-9

2. **Challenge**: It is said that the Book of Revelation is largely a drama of angels. In fact, in this book there are twenty-seven different references to the activities of angels. We will look at a few of them today. After each Scripture reference, share what you understand to be the part played by angels:

✠ *1:1b-2; 22:16*

✠ *1:20; 2:1; 2:8; 2:12; etc.*

✠ *5:11-12; 7:11*

✠ *7:1-4*

✠ *8:3-5*

✠ *8:6, 7, 8, etc.*

✠ *10:1, 2, 6-7*

✠ *15:1*

✠ *18:1, 2*

✝ *21:9-11*

✝ *21:12*

✝ What new appreciation of the ministry of angels do you have after today's study?

Review this week's memory verse.

Day 4

Overview of Revelation 2:18-29

In this section we will be looking at the passage we have studied this week as a whole. The goal is to find the main lessons the Lord has for us from this chapter. Don't worry about being clever or profound—just do your best!

Find the Facts...

1. See if you can state the *content* of this week's passage in a couple of sentences. (Who is speaking, what is taking place, what is the main subject?)

Look for the Heart...

2. What do you think is the main *lesson* of this chapter? (What spiritual truths are taught here? Look for a command, a word of exhortation, a promise, etc.)

LESSON 6

Hear Him Speak ...

3. Look for a *personal application* from the content of this chapter. It should come from the lesson you got from the chapter (question 2). How will you apply the lesson to yourself?

4. Was there a particular verse that ministered to you this week? What was it and how did it minister to you?

LESSON 7
REVELATION 3:1-6

The wealthy and commercially important city of Sardis was located around 30 miles southeast of Thyatira, situated uniquely at the center of a knot of 5 roads, each one leading to other important cities, making it a magnet to draw trade and wealth to itself. Sardis had once been the capital of the kingdom of Lydia and had once had as its king Croesus, whose name became a byword for unimaginable wealth. It was in Sardis that the first coins ever to be minted in Asia Minor were made—making Sardis the birthplace of money as we know it. Today, only a small village named Sart remains on the site of this once-important city.

Sadly, to the church at Sardis Jesus gives no commendation, only condemnation. His letter to them is a *wake-up call*. What a timely word to the church of our day.

Day 1
Read Revelation 3:1-6

And to the angel of the church in Sardis write:
1. With what words did Jesus describe Himself to the church in Sardis? v. 1 Look back and see where this description is found in chapter 1.

    a. Do you remember the significance of the seven Spirits of God? What are the seven stars?

LESSON 7

The number seven speaks of fullness, completion or perfection. Here we see Jesus, the one who has the Holy Spirit in His perfect fullness, saying, *"I know your deeds."* He doesn't say whether their deeds were good or bad—just that He knows them.

2. What profound statement does Jesus make about this particular church? v. 1b

*NAS/NKJ—you have a **name** that you are alive …*
*NIV—you have a **reputation** that you are alive …*

    a. What does it mean to have a *reputation* for something?

    b. What is Jesus saying about this church?

Do you realize that you can *look* like you are alive spiritually (born-again) but not really be, in fact be spiritually dead and doomed for eternity? It is not what you *look like* that matters—it is what you *are*.

The Pharisees *looked* alive. They were the religious leaders of Jesus' day. Certainly the *leaders* were the most spiritual of all, the closest to God … weren't they?

3. In describing the Pharisees, what does Jesus say they were like in Matthew 23:27?

    a. How did they look outwardly? v. 28

    b. What was the truth of the matter? v. 28

    c. Matthew 23:5a helps us to understand. What does it say?

d. What warning does Matthew 6:1 give Pharisee-like people?

4. What prescription does Matthew 6 gives us for the temptation to appear righteous:

   in giving—v.2-4

   in praying—v.5-6

   in fasting—v.16-18

5. **Personal**: Do you do your good deeds to be seen by men or to bring honor and glory to your Father in heaven? The Lord sees all things—He sees *what* we do and He sees *why* we do it. If this is a problem for you and you realize it today—praise God! Ask Him to show you how to *not let your left hand know what your right hand is doing*. Ask Him to help you to be Christ-conscious rather than self-conscious. Some things are hard for us to change by ourselves. Ask God to help you by the power of His Holy Spirit to forget what you look like to others and be careful only that you are approved by Him.

Oswald Chambers says of the apostle Paul, *"Paul is like a musician who does not heed the approval of the audience if he can catch the look of approval from His master."*

This week's memory verse:
"Be diligent to present yourself approved to God ..." 2 Timothy 2:15

Day 2

Read Revelation 3:2-6

Jesus has pronounced judgment on this church of Sardis: *"You are dead."* But there is still hope for this church to wake up and be revived!

1. What is the first word of exhortation given to this slumbering church? v. 2a

NKJ—Be watchful; NAS—Wake up

   a. What do you think it means to *strengthen the things that remain?*

NIV says, *"strengthen what remains and is about to die."* There was yet a flicker of life.

2. Verse 3 gives three more words of exhortation:

   ✦ What were they to *remember*? What do you think this means?

   ✦ What were they to *keep*, hold fast, or obey?

   ✦ What final exhortation does verse 3 give?

3. **Personal**: If, as you have been studying this letter to Sardis, you have been convicted of being one who *looks* spiritually alive but you know in your heart that your spiritual life is far from what it appears to be—or if you simply feel the need for *spiritual revival*—apply these words to your own life:

   ✣ Wake up!

   ✣ Remember!

   ✣ Obey!

   ✣ Repent!

4. What would happen if they did not *wake up?* v. 3b

Although this word of Jesus is probably not referring to the Second Coming but rather to His coming against this particular church, or opposing them in judgment, still when we read it we naturally think of the *"day of the Lord (which) will come just like a thief in the night" (1 Thessalonians 5:2).*

This church—which looked alive but was really dead—was setting itself up for judgment. When Jesus comes again it will be in judgment. The question must be asked, are we ready? What we do with this passage may well give us our answer. To this dead church Jesus says:

"Rouse yourselves and keep awake, and strengthen and invigorate what remains ... so call to mind the lessons you received and heard; continually lay them to heart and obey them and repent. In case you will not rouse yourselves and keep awake and watch, I will come upon you like a thief and you will not know or suspect at what hour I come." Revelation 3:2-3 Amplified

a. **Personal**: What will the Lord's coming be for you? Will it be like a thief in the night—a coming in judgment, or will it be the culmination of what you have believed and lived for?

5. Were there any true believers left in Sardis? v. 4 How does Jesus describe them?

    a. What would their reward be? Why?

    b. Read the beautiful account given in Revelation 7:9-17. How does verse 14 say the robes were made white?

    c. Apply this thought to yourself—will you be dressed in white? Why?

6. What three things did Jesus say about those who overcome? v. 5

In Matthew 10:32, 33, Jesus says, *"Everyone therefore who shall confess Me before men, I will also confess him before My Father who is in heaven. But whoever shall deny Me before men, I will also deny him before My Father who is in heaven."*

Overcomers are ones who, by their lives and by their words, confess that Jesus is Lord!

Review this week's memory verse.

Day 3: "Sevens" in Revelation

Halley's Bible Handbook states that the Book of Revelation *"is built around a system of 'sevens.'"* And Henry M. Morris in his commentary on Revelation says, *"A unique aspect of the Book of Revelation ... is its remarkable 'sevenness.'"* Some of the "sevens" are as follows:

- 7 letters (1-3)
- 7 churches (1:4)
- 7 spirits (1:4)
- 7 candlesticks (1:12)
- 7 stars (1:16)
- 7 lamps (4:5)
- 7 seals (5:1)
- 7 horns (5:6)
- 7 eyes (5:6)
- 7 angels (8:2)
- 7 trumpets (8:2)
- 7 thunders (10:3)
- 7 thousand (11:13)
- 7 heads (12:3)
- 7 crowns (12:3)
- 7 plagues (15:1)
- 7 bowls (15:7)
- 7 mountains (17:9)
- 7 kings (17:10)

If we were to look carefully, we would also find in the Book of Revelation that there are: seven beatitudes, seven years of judgment, seven divisions in each of the letters to the seven churches, seven "I Ams" of Christ, and seven doxologies in heaven.

The number 7 is seen throughout the whole Bible. Other examples of "7s" in the Bible are: the Sabbath day is the 7th day, the Levitical system is based on a cycle of 7s—every 7th day a Sabbath day, every 7th year a Sabbatical year (a year of rest for the land), every 7th Sabbatical year followed by a year of Jubilee (debts canceled, slaves set free, lands returned), every 7th month had 3 holy feasts, 7 weeks between Passover and Pentecost, Passover feast lasted 7 days, Tabernacles feast lasted 7 days, even in the offerings of the important holy days—14 (2x7) lambs offered at Passover; 14 lambs and 70 (10x7) bulls offered at the Feast of Tabernacles, 7 lambs at Pentecost.

The Bible begins with 7 days of Creation and ends with a book in which the number 7 appears more than in all the other New Testament books combined. Why? The answer most likely lies in the fact that the Book of Revelation is the climactic book of the Bible—the number 7 being the number regarded as representing completion or fullness. The Book of Revelation, written by the last of the Apostles at the end of the Apostolic Age, focuses on the events that will bring God's work, which was begun at Creation, to completion and fullness.

Today in our study we will look at two of the unique "7s" of Revelation:

✣ The 7 Beatitudes: *Write the condition of the blessing promised in each of the following Revelation verses (we will make each one personal):*

✣ 1:3—Blessed is she ...

✣ 14:13—Blessed is she ...

REVELATION

- 16:15—Blessed is she ...

- 19:9—Blessed is she ...

- 20:6—Blessed is she ...

- 22:7—Blessed is she ...

- 22:14—Blessed is she ...

- What hope do these verses give you as you consider the final days in which we live?

- The 7 "I Ams": In the following statements in Revelation, we will see Christ as He is! Write after each one the name or characteristic Jesus claims:

- 1:8—I Am ...

- 1:17—I Am ...

- 1:18—I Am ...

- 2:23—I Am ...

- 21:6—I Am ...

- 22:13—I Am ...

- 22:16—I Am ...

✣ *What "I Am" gives you the ability to see who Jesus is most clearly?*

Review this week's memory verse.

Information in today's lesson has been gleaned from "Halley's Bible Handbook" and H.M. Morris', "The Revelation Record."

Day 4

Overview of Revelation 3:1-6

In this section we will be looking at the passage we have studied this week as a whole. The goal is to find the main lessons the Lord has for us from this chapter. Don't worry about being clever or profound—just do your best!

Find the Facts...

1. See if you can state the *content* of this week's passage in a couple of sentences. (Who is speaking, what is taking place, what is the main subject?)

Look for the Heart...

2. What do you think is the main *lesson* of this chapter? (What spiritual truths are taught here? Look for a command, a word of exhortation, a promise, etc.)

Hear Him Speak ...

3. Look for a *personal application* from the content of this chapter. It should come from the lesson you got from the chapter (question 2). How will you apply the lesson to yourself?

4. Was there a particular verse that ministered to you this week? What was it and how did it minister to you?

LESSON 8
REVELATION 3:7-13

Silence in heaven—everything stops! For a half-hour there is no praise, no joyous worship, just a pregnant pause as a hush falls across the heavenlies and brings a brief respite on earth. Why an interlude at this point? Because our gracious God is giving mankind a moment to consider his plight and turn to Christ before the seventh seal is opened and the trumpet judgments begin. The trumpet judgments will take place very near to the end of the Tribulation period.

Henry M. Morris calls the church in Philadelphia, "The church of the open door;" Warren Wiersbe calls it "The faithful church," noting that, although it was not a large or strong church, it was a faithful one; and Tim LaHaye belovedly calls it "The church Christ loved." Only two of the seven churches received no rebuke from Christ, Smyrna was one, Philadelphia the other. It's interesting that both of these churches were small and weak in the sight of the world and yet greatly honored by God. How often we attempt to be great and successful in the sight of the world, while neglecting the assessment of God. What an example these churches are to us—let us continue as we study to be careful to *"hear what the Spirit says to the churches."*

Day 1
Read Revelation 3:7-13

And to the angel of the church in Philadelphia write:
1. Share the 4-part description of Jesus found in verse 7.

This is the first time in the letters to the churches that the salutation of Jesus isn't found in His description as given in chapter 1. The titles Jesus uses here give us four aspects of His character. The keys of David represent His authority.

    a. What other keys do we see belonging to Jesus?

Matthew 16:19
Revelation 1:18

    b. What ability does the one with the keys have according to verse 7?

According to commentators, Philadelphia was a lesser city than the others addressed in these letters, but right away we see that this makes no difference. Jesus is the one in control! He is the one with the keys! He decides which doors will be opened and which ones will be closed!

    c. How does this fact give you a new perspective in your own situation?

Jesus doesn't say what their deeds are—He simply says, *"I know your deeds."* We've already recognized that no rebuke is given to this church—instead it is a letter full of promises!

2. What is the *first* promise He makes to them? v.8

    a. Jesus gives three reasons for this promise in verse 8.
        1)
        2)
        3)

*NKJ—for you have **a little strength***
*NAS—because you have **a little power***
*NIV—I know that you have **little strength***
*Amp.—I know that you have **but little power***

Whether they had *a little strength* or *little strength*, either way, this was a weak church—yet one that proved to be faithful, keeping His Word in a time of great persecution and not denying His name when the cost was great.

3. We often think it is so important that we *look* strong and full of power as Christians. Consider this picture of a weak church that is given an open door that no man can shut. What are we taught in 2 Corinthians 12:9 about our weakness and God's power?

    a. The blessed words of 2 Corinthians 12:10 are: *"... for when I am weak, then I am strong."* Is this a principle that you understand? How does this help you in your personal place of weakness today?

Have you been tempted to think that it all depends on *you*—on your position, on your strength, on your power and influence? Satan tempts us to think these thoughts, and it isn't hard for him to do, because we are naturally prone to think this way. In the world, everything does depend on our strength—it is only in the work of God that *weakness* is a prerequisite! One commentator on this portion of Scripture said this: *"God had warned the Churches of Ephesus and Sardis against boasting of their influential standing. Here, He cautions the Church of Philadelphia not to be discouraged because they are a nobody; for God is not dependant on worldly prestige."*

This week's memory verse:
"Not by might, nor by power, but by My Spirit, says the Lord ..."
Zechariah 4:6b

Day 2

Read Revelation 3:9-13

The first promise made to the church in Philadelphia was an open door for ministry. Actually, Philadelphia was originally founded to be a missionary city—to bring to the barbarous regions of Phrygia the culture and civilization of Hellenism (Greek thought and ideals). How like the Lord to take this city with its purpose for spreading Hellenism and give it an open door through the church to spread the gospel of Jesus Christ!

1. What is the *second* thing promised to this church in Philadelphia? v. 9

The trouble for Christians at this time came not only from the Romans but also from the Jews—who shut the doors of the synagogue on any who proclaimed the name of Christ. Jesus says of these Judaizers that they are of the synagogue of Satan and that they are not truly Jews, because they reject the very Son of God, as well as those who believe on His name.

   a. Have you ever been rejected and *shut out* because of your beliefs as a Christian? How does it give you patience to endure when you realize that those who have persecuted you will one day ...

   ✝ *bow down at your feet* (in acquiescence to your correct belief)?

   ✝ *know that He has loved you?*

LESSON 8

2. What is the *third* promise that Jesus makes to this persecuted church? v. 10

   a. To what do you think *the hour of testing* refers?

   b. How does Matthew 24:21 describe this period?

The hour of testing is described in detail in Revelation chapters 6 through 19. It is the 7-year period of tribulation, which severely tests the whole world, prior to the Second Coming of Christ to the earth. It is a judgment of the *world* and not the *church,* and therefore, according to the promise given here, the church will be spared. Believers know this promise as *the Rapture of the Church.* This portion of Scripture makes it appear that the Rapture will occur *before* the Tribulation: *"I will save you from the hour of testing ..."*

3. Read about this wondrous event in 1 Thessalonians 4:16-17. What will take place?

   a. What does 1 Corinthians 15:52 add to this description?

Chuck Smith sees the Rapture as taking place in Revelation 4:1, where it says, *after these things*. He says that *after these things*— after the things of the Church—after the Church has finished her testimony upon the earth and God is through with us, *"there shall come from heaven the voice of the archangel, and the trump of God: and the dead in Christ shall rise first: then we which are alive and remain shall be caught up together with them in the clouds, to meet the Lord in the air: and so shall we ever be with the Lord."*

4. John 14:1-3 speaks of this glorious event. Read these words and consider:

    ✝ What does it do for you personally to consider the Rapture of the Church?

    ✝ Have you thanked the Lord for the wonderful provision He has made for His church?

5. When is Jesus coming? Revelation 3:11

    a. What must we do while we wait? What do you think this means?

    b. What is another thing we are told to do while we wait? Luke 19:13 What do you think this means? (Are you doing it?)

Jesus speaks in verse 11 of the possibility of losing one's crown. We cannot lose our salvation, but we are able to lose our rewards. After the Rapture, the church will celebrate the marriage supper (Revelation 19:7-9), and then be rewarded (1 Corinthians 3:12-15), and later return to earth with Christ when He comes again to set up His kingdom (Revelation 19:11-20:6)!

6. What promises are made to the one who overcomes? v. 12
    1)
    2)
    3)
    4)

Of the pillar in the temple, Warren Wiersbe says this: *"God's pillars are not made of stone, because there is no temple in the heavenly city (21:22). His pillars are faithful people who bear His name for His glory ..."* Will you be a pillar in the temple of God?

Review this week's memory verse.

Day 3: Christ in Revelation

Throughout the Book of Revelation, we are given a magnificent presentation of Jesus Christ in all His risen glory. We remember that the Book of Revelation is an *apocalyptic* book. The word *apocalypse* is the Greek word for *revelation* and means *uncovering, revealing,* or *unveiling.* It is an unveiling *of that which otherwise could not be known.* It is the unveiling of Jesus Christ— *"The Revelation of Jesus Christ"* (Revelation 1:1). It is *"God's final unveiling of the glories of His blessed Son"* (Charles Feinburg).

One of the ways in which Jesus is *unveiled* in the Book of Revelation is through the many names given Him in this book.

1. From each of the following Revelation verses, write the name, title or description given Jesus. (In some of these verses there are several names given—see if you can get them all!)

    1:5

    1:8

    1:17

    1:18

2:18

3:7

3:14

5:5

13:8

19:11

19:13

19:16

22:16

2. Read the description of Jesus given in Isaiah 53:2-3, and share what you learn about Jesus in His first coming.

   a. We know that in Revelation we are seeing the *resurrected Christ*—but wasn't Jesus always the Alpha and the Omega, the First and the Last? How does Philippians 2:6-7 help us to understand what took place during the first advent of Christ.

   b. How will Jesus appear in His Second coming? Luke 21:27

Review this week's memory verse.

Day 4
Overview of Revelation 3:7-13

In this section we will be looking at the passage we have studied this week as a whole. The goal is to find the main lessons the Lord has for us from this chapter. Don't worry about being clever or profound—just do your best!

Find the Facts...

1. See if you can state the *content* of this week's passage in a couple of sentences. (Who is speaking, what is taking place, what is the main subject?)

Look for the Heart...

2. What do you think is the main *lesson* of this chapter? (What spiritual truths are taught here? Look for a command, a word of exhortation, a promise, etc.)

Hear Him Speak...

3. Look for a *personal application* from the content of this chapter. It should come from the lesson you got from the chapter (question 2). How will you apply the lesson to yourself?

4. Was there a particular verse that ministered to you this week? What was it and how did it minister to you?

LESSON 9
REVELATION 3:14-22

When we first read the letter to the church in Laodicea, it would seem that this is a church that Jesus *hated*. But we are reminded very quickly in this passage of the fact that *those Jesus loves He reproves*. Laodicea was a church that had turned from trusting Christ to trusting themselves. They were a wealthy church in a wealthy city. They had all the right plans and programs, but they didn't have fellowship with Christ, and they received no commendation from Him. The call came to Laodicea that has come to every church preceding her in these letters: *repent!* The grace of God is seen in that the very ones who He is about to spew out of His mouth are invited to sit with Him on His throne. That is truly amazing grace!

Day 1
Read Revelation 3:14-22

And to the angel of the church in Laodicea write:
1. Share the 3-part description of Jesus given to the church in Laodicea.
    1)
    2)
    3)

In this verse, we see that Jesus is the beginning and end of all things. He is the beginning of the creation …

   a. What are we taught about this in John 1:3?

b. What does Colossians 1:16-17 say about this?

And He is the final word of God—in Jesus, God says, "Amen."

   c. The word amen in the Hebrew means true, and it carries with it the idea of finality. How do you see Jesus as God's Amen?

2. What did Jesus know about this church? v. 15

   a. What was His appraisal of their condition? v. 16

   b. **Challenge:** The church at Sardis was cold and dead; the church at Laodicea was lukewarm—Jesus preferred the church at Sardis. Why do you think Jesus would prefer a cold church (or individual) over a church (or individual) that is lukewarm?

3. Jesus gives the reason for their lukewarm condition in verse 17. What did He say was their state of mind?

   a. The possession of riches gives the false allusion of security and lack of need. The person with money sees himself in a position of being able to buy anything that he might need. But there are some things that cannot be bought. Take a moment and think—what are some of them?

b. There are some very strong words in Scripture over the love of both money and the things of this world. Look at these verses and share what you learn:

Matthew 6:24

James 4:4

1 John 2:15

c. What simple truth are we given in Proverbs 23:4? How does this verse help you personally?

Money can never take the place of spiritual power. We cannot *buy* spiritual fruit. A church can have committees, programs, agendas, and services, without doing anything of lasting value in the spiritual realm. That is the state of this church in Laodicea.

4. Jesus gives us the formula for bearing real spiritual fruit in John 15:4-5. Read these verses and answer these questions:

   a. How is it that we bear fruit?

   b. What can we do apart from Jesus?

This week's memory verse
"...Apart from Me you can do nothing." John 15:5

Day 2

Read Revelation 3:17-22

1. What, again, was the perspective Laodicea had about themselves? v.17

   a. Is this how Jesus saw them? Share His perspective on the church at Laodicea.

It is so interesting to compare this church to the beloved church at Smyrna. These two churches give us such a vivid perspective on God's unique perception of things. The church that was poor, He calls rich; the church that is rich (in earthly things), He calls poor. He looks at things with a spiritual, eternal viewpoint—never one that is limited to the temporal.

   b. Have you learned to look at things from an eternal perspective? In the eternal, where do you stand—are you rich or are you poor? See what 2 Corinthians 4:18 says on this subject.

2. Jesus' counsel to this mistaken church is in direct relation to their need. From verse 18:

   ✤ Because spiritually they were *poor,* what should they do?

   ✤ Because spiritually they were *naked,* what should they do?

   ✤ Because spiritually they were *blind,* what should they do?

LESSON 9

Each one of these words of Jesus happens to apply to the actual (not just spiritual) condition of Laodicea. They were wealthy – but they needed something money couldn't buy—they needed life from Jesus. The city of Laodicea was known for its black wool and garment industry, but spiritually they were naked—they needed to be clothed with His garments of righteousness. Laodicea was famous all over the world for making a medicinal eye powder for weak and ailing eyes—but Jesus said they were blind—they needed to receive spiritual sight from Him.

    a. **Personal**: Read the word given by the prophet Isaiah in Isaiah 55:1-2. Do you find yourself spending money to buy that which does not satisfy? How can we find life and satisfaction?

3. What does Jesus say in verse 19a, by way of explanation for all He has said to this church so far?

How beautiful these words must have sounded to those who would read this letter. *Jesus loved them!*

    a. Read Hebrews 12:7-11, which speaks of the discipline of the Lord.

    ✚ Who does God discipline? (v. 7)

    ✚ What are those without discipline? (v. 8)

    ✚ Why does God discipline us? (v. 10)

    ✚ What is the result for us? (v. 11)

b. **Personal**: Have you ever experienced the discipline of the Lord? Are you experiencing it right now? How do these verses encourage you?

Jesus' word to them is *be zealous therefore, and repent.*

c. **Personal**: If you have seen yourself in this church: neither hot nor cold but lukewarm, trusting in yourself rather than Christ, this is His word to *you*. Don't disregard the severity of His words in verse 16. Be thankful for the exhortation in verse 19. Turn from your false sense of self-sufficiency and apathy, be zealous for your Savior, turn your thoughts to Christ and repent.

Verse 20 is the invitation. Christ is standing outside of the church! Amazing! How many churches are going on about their business, with Christ standing on the outside? How many Christians are doing the same thing? Oftentimes this verse is used as an invitation to bring unsaved people to Christ—and it is useful in that case, but here we see Jesus standing outside of the church, wanting to be invited in.

4. What is promised to the one who invites Jesus in?

This Scripture speaks of fellowship. A church or a Christian operating in the flesh has no *fellowship* with Christ. This verse also speaks of His imminent personal return.

a. Share the words of Jesus in Matthew 24:33.

b. What ultimate invitation is given to everyone who believes in Christ as Lord and is united to Him in heaven forever? Revelation 19:9

5. What is promised to the ones who overcome? Rev. 3:21 (Notice who is our example in overcoming and where He is now!)

What an amazing promise—what amazing grace!

Review this week's memory verse.

Day 3: Jesus' Words to the 7 Churches

One of the unique aspects of the letters to the seven churches is that these letters were written with a pattern. Each one begins with a characteristic of Christ, followed by a word of commendation, following the commendation Christ then rebukes His church for their errors, He then speaks a word of exhortation, and finally He leaves each church with a promise.

1. **Challenge**: Fill in the following chart from the verses given. Finish this exercise using *you* as the one being spoken to. What characteristic of Christ most speaks to you, what commendation do you feel He gives you, with what word do you find yourself convicted, what word of exhortation challenges and encourages you in your Christianity, and what promise is most significant to you personally? Have fun with this! Let Christ speak His word to you today.

Ephesus (Revelation 2:1-7)
- ✟ *Characteristic of Christ*
- ✟ *Commendation*
- ✟ *Condemnation*
- ✟ *Exhortation*
- ✟ *Promise*

Smyrna (Revelation 2:8-11)
- ✟ *Characteristic of Christ*
- ✟ *Commendation*
- ✟ *Condemnation* – none given
- ✟ *Exhortation*
- ✟ *Promise*

Pergamum (Revelation 2:12-17)
- ✟ *Characteristic of Christ*
- ✟ *Commendation*
- ✟ *Condemnation*
- ✟ *Exhortation*
- ✟ *Promise*

Thyatira (Revelation 2:18-29)
- ✟ *Characteristic of Christ*
- ✟ *Commendation*
- ✟ *Condemnation*
- ✟ *Exhortation*
- ✟ *Promise*

Sardis (Revelation 3:1-6)
- ✟ *Characteristic of Christ*
- ✟ *Commendation* – none given
- ✟ *Condemnation*
- ✟ *Exhortation*
- ✟ *Promise*

Philadelphia (Revelation 3:7-13)
- ✝ *Characteristic of Christ*
- ✝ *Commendation*
- ✝ *Condemnation* – none given
- ✝ *Exhortation*
- ✝ *Promise*

Laodicea (Revelation 3:14-22)
- ✝ *Characteristic of Christ*
- ✝ *Commendation* – none given
- ✝ *Condemnation*
- ✝ *Exhortation*
- ✝ *Promise*

You!
- ✝ *Characteristic of Christ*
- ✝ *Commendation*
- ✝ *Condemnation*
- ✝ *Exhortation*
- ✝ *Promise*

2. An interesting thing about the promises spoken to overcomers is that in all seven cases they are mentioned again in the final pages of Revelation in the description given of the glory to come. Finish your lesson with this wonderful picture:

The tree of life promised to Ephesus …
- ✝ *Revelation 22:2*

Deliverance from the second death promised to Smyrna …
- ✝ *Revelation 20:6*

The new name promised to Pergamum …
✝ *Revelation 22:4*

The morning star promised to Thyatira …
✝ *Revelation 22:16*

The white raiment promised to Sardis …
✝ *Revelation 19:8, 14*

The new Jerusalem promised to Philadelphia …
✝ *Revelation 21:2*

Sharing His throne promised to Laodicea …
✝ *Revelation 20:4.*

Review this week's memory verse.

Day 4

Overview of Revelation 3:14-22

In this section we will be looking at the passage we have studied this week as a whole. The goal is to find the main lessons the Lord has for us from this chapter. Don't worry about being clever or profound—just do your best!

Find the Facts …

1. See if you can state the *content* of this week's passage in a couple of sentences. (Who is speaking, what is taking place, what is the main subject?)

LESSON 9

Look for the Heart...

2. What do you think is the main *lesson* of this chapter? (What spiritual truths are taught here? Look for a command, a word of exhortation, a promise, etc.)

Hear Him Speak...

3. Look for a *personal application* from the content of this chapter. It should come from the lesson you got from the chapter (question 2). How will you apply the lesson to yourself?

4. Was there a particular verse that ministered to you this week? What was it and how did it minister to you?

ABOUT THE AUTHOR

Linda has dedicated her life to serving the Lord as a teacher, writer, and speaker. While teaching the Word of God, training leaders, and speaking at retreats and other women's ministry functions, she has also written curriculum for over 20 books of the Bible.

If you would be interested in having more information about her ministry, please visit her blog at www.lindaoborne.wordpress.com, or email her at myutmost1@aol.com.

www.ingramcontent.com/pod-product-compliance
Lightning Source LLC
Chambersburg PA
CBHW071308040426
42444CB00009B/1918